# SKIING

*A Guide to the Colorado High Country*

Jeff Andrew                    COPPER MOUNTAIN

**A RENAISSANCE HOUSE PUBLICATION**

©Copyright 1987 by Eleanor H. Ayer. Printed in the United States of America. All rights reserved. This book or any parts thereof, may not be reproduced in any manner whatsoever without written permission of the publisher.

ISBN: 0-939650-73-8

**RENAISSANCE HOUSE**
A Division of Jende-Hagan, Inc.
541 Oak Street ~ P.O. Box 177
Frederick, CO 80530

Cover photo courtesy
Jeff Andrew, Copper Mountain

Nathan Bilow, Monarch Ski Area

# WELCOME

Along the chain of the Rocky Mountains, which runs from Canada to New Mexico, the mountains in Colorado are the highest--53 peaks over 14,000 feet high and more than a thousand over 10,000 feet. It's been said that if you took a flatiron to Colorado, it would press out to a state the size of Texas. (But since that would irritate the Texans, no one has yet tried it!)

This **Colorado Traveler** describes the mountains developed for alpine skiing and offers a sampling of Nordic trails; check with local sports shops and chambers of commerce for other suggestions on cross-country ski routes. To learn more about Colorado's entire mountain system, check the **Colorado Traveler** volume *Mountains and Passes*. Other good books on Colorado skiing include *Central Colorado Ski Tours,* by Tom and Sanse Sudduth; *Ski Tracks in the Rockies: A Century of Skiing in Colorado,* by Abbott Fay; *It's Easy, Edna, It's Downhill All the Way,* by Edna Dercum; *I Never Look Back: The Story of Buddy Werner,* by John Rolfe Burroughs; and *Mountain Troops: Camp Hale, Colorado,* by Winston Pote. Our thanks to the Colorado Ski Museum in Vail (p. 43) for providing a nice selection of historic photos of Colorado skiing.

# Contents

In The Beginning . . . . . . . . . . . . . . . . . . . . . . . . 4
Colorado Ski Country USA . . . . . . . . . . . . . . . . . . . 13
Aspen Mountain . . . . . . . . . . . . . . . . . . . . . . . . 14
Buttermilk . . . . . . . . . . . . . . . . . . . . . . . . . . . 15
Snowmass . . . . . . . . . . . . . . . . . . . . . . . . . . . 16
Aspen Highlands . . . . . . . . . . . . . . . . . . . . . . . . 17
Vail / Beaver Creek . . . . . . . . . . . . . . . . . . . . . . . 18
Keystone . . . . . . . . . . . . . . . . . . . . . . . . . . . . 20
Copper Mountain . . . . . . . . . . . . . . . . . . . . . . . 22
Map of Colorado . . . . . . . . . . . . . . . . . . . . . . . . 24
Breckenridge . . . . . . . . . . . . . . . . . . . . . . . . . . 26
Winter Park . . . . . . . . . . . . . . . . . . . . . . . . . . . 28
Steamboat . . . . . . . . . . . . . . . . . . . . . . . . . . . 30
Loveland . . . . . . . . . . . . . . . . . . . . . . . . . . . . 32
Crested Butte / Ski Estes Park . . . . . . . . . . . . . . . . . 34
Telluride . . . . . . . . . . . . . . . . . . . . . . . . . . . . 35
Wolf Creek / Berthoud . . . . . . . . . . . . . . . . . . . . . 36
Purgatory . . . . . . . . . . . . . . . . . . . . . . . . . . . . 37
Silver Creek / Ski Cooper . . . . . . . . . . . . . . . . . . . 38
Ski Sunlight . . . . . . . . . . . . . . . . . . . . . . . . . . 39
Monarch . . . . . . . . . . . . . . . . . . . . . . . . . . . . 40
Conquistador . . . . . . . . . . . . . . . . . . . . . . . . . . 41
Powderhorn . . . . . . . . . . . . . . . . . . . . . . . . . . 42
Colorado Ski Museum . . . . . . . . . . . . . . . . . . . . . 43
Cross-Country . . . . . . . . . . . . . . . . . . . . . . . . . 44
Names & Numbers . . . . . . . . . . . . . . . . . . . . . . . 46
U.S. Olympic Committee . . . . . . . . . . . . . . . . . . . 48

Colorado Ski Museum  SKIING 6,000 YEARS AGO

# IN THE BEGINNING

Whether you prefer alpine or cross-country skiing, your sport began not as a recreation, but as a necessary form of transportation. Snowshoe Thompson, (*nee* John A. Thorenson) was the Johnny Appleseed of skiing. Snowshoe earned his name not from today's webbed variety of winter foot gear, but from the earliest skis, cumbersome wooden slabs made of rough wood, called snowshoes. With these contraptions attached to each foot by a strap, Snowshoe skiied the Rockies and Sierra Nevadas, delivering the mail. Thompson was not the first; a Frank Bishop shows up in mountain mail annals previously, but Snowshoe is most often remembered.

The word ski is derived from a Norwegian word which means "two boards." It was the early Norsemen who first developed the hardware, by slicing crude wood into slats. That done, they created a god and goddess of skiing to watch over them while they utilized their equipment. Instead of two poles of bamboo or aluminum, outfitted with baskets to keep them atop the snow, these early skiers carried one long, heavy pole for balance. On particularly steep slopes, skiers might stick the pole between their legs as a brake.

Colorado Ski Museum    OURAY MAIL CARRIER, 1912

The toughest part of hand-crafting skis in the early days was getting the tips to curve upward, a feat accomplished by a process of steaming and bending the wood. Purposely, the skis were often cut to different lengths, the longer one intended as a base, and the shorter one used for steering. Averaging ten feet in length, these unwieldy attachments were almost an inch thick, and about five inches across.

Skiing was first recorded in Colorado in 1857. Jim Baker, former mountain man, trapper, and guide, was leading an expedition into the territory from Utah, when he and his party became lost. Fashioning a pair of skis, he climbed to an overlook, from which he could reconnoiter the expedition and resume his course to Fort Massachusetts in southern Colorado.

When the gold seekers arrived for the 1858-59 rush, they used every means including skis in pursuit of their fortunes. For better uphill traction, the miners sometimes attached fur strips to the bottoms of their skis. The sky pilots were no less daring. Father John Dyer, based in the Breckenridge area, was one of the best-known skiing ministers. He would regularly traverse rugged Mosquito Pass to conduct services in Fairplay and the South Park area, delivering mail along the way. Early doctors used skis, and even cowboys would strap on the boards to seek out cattle lost in a blizzard.

Colorado Ski Museum     CARL HOWELSEN, 1915

As skiing evolved from necessity to recreation, contests and competition entered the picture. There is record in 1883, of the miners in Irwin (later a ghost town) organizing a racing club. Three years later, downhill competitions were held at Crested Butte, although its development as a ski area was still years away. Because of the primitive state of bindings, jumping competition was not yet too popular. Stories prevail, however, of a daring skier (or madman) who would wait on a hill above a canyon for the D&RG train *en route* from Gunnison to Crested Butte. His aim--to jump the moving engine on skis!

The first organized jumping competition was not recorded until 1912, when the little town of Hot Sulphur Springs hosted the West's first winter carnival. Two years later, Steamboat Springs followed suit, under the organization of Norwegian Carl Howelsen. The carnival is still an annual event, and Steamboat has become a home for international ski champs. By 1919, the Colorado Mountain Club had completed a ski jump on Genesee Mountain, west of Denver, and the following year, ski pros nationwide met there for competition. Ski clubs were mushrooming throughout the state.

With the completion of the Moffat Railroad Tunnel in 1927, the Arlberg Club of Denver put in a bid for the cabins used by the construction crew at the tunnel's

Colorado Ski Museum  WINTER PARK SKI TRAIN, 1940

west portal. They cut ski runs on the adjacent mountain, and offered train transportation round-trip from Denver for $2.25--the humble beginnings of the Winter Park ski area.

Technology and necessity improved the quality of ski hardware; by the mid-30s, cable bindings and metal edges were standard equipment. The state's first rope tow was installed in 1937 at a small area atop Berthoud Pass, a gift of the May Co. department store. The following season, the area claimed 50,000 skier days.

With the pressure on to provide uphill luxury for skiers, Winter Park installed a T-Bar. Innovative, but destined to extinction was the "boat tow" devised by the Roaring Fork ski club. This Aspen group proposed to carry skiers up Ajax Mountain on two long sleds, poised side-by-side atop an old mine hoist. Steamboat tried a similar system, but it was the Gunnison ski club that claimed the state's first chair lift. Completed in 1939, this conveyance used chairs and cable from a nearby abandoned mine. The Pikes Peak ski club near Colorado Springs, shuttled skiers uphill on a rope tow powered by a Model A Ford.

About this time, night skiing came into vogue. The Climax Molybdenum Mine near Leadville developed a lighted area. On Howelsen Hill at Steamboat Springs, illumination was provided by car lights.

Colorado Ski Museum  SKIING DOWN THE SAND DUNES, 1930s

As America moved toward war, Colorado skiing once again became a utilitarian endeavor. Based on the Finns' success at withstanding a Russian attack on their homeland by the use of armored ski troops, the United States organized a similar unit, subsequently called the Tenth Mountain Division. The ghost town of Pando, Colorado, was ultimately selected as the training camp, and was soon renamed Camp Hale, in honor of Denver's Brigadier General Irving Hale. Pando was a decidedly scenic spot at 9,200 feet, with adequate rail facilities. Frequent temperatures of -40 degrees made it an excellent training ground for the troops.

Leadville being the major town closest to Camp Hale, it was the natural place for R&R. But because of its wild reputation, the army made it off limits to troops. By early 1942, Leadville had taken steps to clean up its sanitation regulations and had enacted legislation against prostitution. By this time, though, the soldiers had made Aspen their playground, a preference that remained even after the war.

The troops trained in white--white skis, white suits, a camouflage for the conditions under which they would be fighting. The major downhill run started at the top of Tennessee Pass, accessed by what was, at that time, the world's longest T-Bar. In 1944, the combat-ready division was sent to Italy. There, at Riva

Colorado Ski Museum                  TENTH MOUNTAIN DIVISION

Ridge, high above the Po River Valley, the Tenth Mountain Division lost 992 men in a successful battle against the Axis. Today, a run at Vail is named Riva Ridge, in honor of those men of the Tenth.

At war's end, much of the equipment from Camp Hale was moved to Fort Carson near Colorado Springs. By July, 1965, the army had ordered remaining facilities at the camp to be disposed of by the GSA. Today, a monument on Tennessee Pass lists those killed in action from the Tenth. The Division hosts frequent reunions at Vail and throughout the nation.

Addicted by the end of the war to the ritual of daily skiing, many members of the Tenth returned to Colorado to work in ski-related businesses, helping establish recreational skiing as a major industry in the state. One such was Friedl Pfeifer, a native Austrian who had joined American forces as a ski instructor for the Tenth. While recuperating in a California hospital, he was contacted by the Paepckes (of container corporation fame) who loved Aspen and proposed to make it a ski center. Pfeifer, who shared this love of Aspen, agreed to assist in this massive endeavor. With the help of project manager Herbert Bayer, himself a refugee from Austria, two chair lifts were erected, the one serving Ajax Mountain being the world's longest at that time. They organized a ski patrol, and by January 11,

Colorado Ski Museum
## Max Dercum

Colorado Ski Museum
## Edna Dercum

1947, had prepared for the grand opening of the area. As the bigwigs from Denver arrived, they were met with a torchlight reception, bands, and a color guard of Tenth Mountain Division vets. There was only one problem--virtually no snow! But the show went on, and Paepcke went on to develop Aspen into a center of culture as well as skiing, through his Aspen Institute for Humanistic Studies. The winter of 1949 saw Aspen host the FIS (Federation Internationale de Ski) world championships. The once-famed silver mining town was back on the map as a year-round attraction.

Arapahoe Basin, known after 1972 as A Basin, was also a product of the post-war ski boom. In 1946, planners recruited an army truck to shuttle skiers between the lodge and a rope tow which started them on their way up the mountain. Over the next two seasons, two chair lifts were installed, which accommodated 13,000 skiers. A pioneer in ski programs for the handicapped, A Basin hosted the first ski competition for senior citizens and instituted an amputee program.

Today, A Basin and Keystone operate under the same umbrella, but this was not always so. Max Dercum, once a professor of forestry in Pennsylvania, was a ski instructor at A Basin and owned a small adjacent lodge. Max had skied nearby Keystone Mountain many times, and his retirement dream was to develop a ski area there. Teaming with other interested entrepreneurs and the Ralston Purina Co., Dercum supervised the design and construction of the area in an ecologically sound manner. One of Colorado's newest areas, Keystone, officially opened in 1970.

Another relatively late bloomer that now dominates much of the Colorado ski scene was Vail. Earl Eaton, a

Colorado Ski Museum        BERTHOUD PASS SKI AREA, 1942

latter-day prospector looking to capitalize on the early '50s uranium boom, became side-tracked when he surveyed Vail Mountain. In company with Pete Seibert, Eaton set out on a long and frustrating bureaucratic road to secure the government permits necessary to opening a ski area. Investments from the Quaker Company, Schlitz, Sears Roebuck and other giants helped fund the new area. By December, 1962, Vail was ready to open, advertising America's first gondola lift and two double chairs. Former President Gerald Ford was among those contributing to Vail's publicity, promotion which has made it one of the highest profile areas in the country.

With the growth of skiing in Colorado following World War II, promoters began looking to the state as a potential Olympic site. As early as 1967, a committee was organized to prepare a proposal for the 1976 Winter Olympics. There were rumblings from the opposition who complained that Denver and Colorado were not prepared for the crowds that such an event would draw. Transportation and lodging were inadequate, they said, but the plans went forward. The last straw for the opposition was the committee's proposal of Evergreen for cross-country events. This foothills town just west of Denver had erratic snowfall at best,

Colorado Ski Museum  BUDDY WERNER, 1964

and many found the proposed site preposterous. The now-organized opposition, calling itself *Citizens for Colorado's Future,* lobbied long and hard, ultimately sending the question to the voters. The citizens voted resoundingly: NO OLYMPICS IN COLORADO!

Perhaps best-known of Colorado's ski champions is Steamboat's Wallace "Buddy" Werner, an Olympian in 1956 and 1964, who was killed in an avalanche in Switzerland in 1964. His sister, Gladys "Skeeter" Werner was a 1956 Olympian. (See **Colorado Traveler** volume *Hall of Fame.*) Perhaps Colorado's finest all-around skier, Steamboat champ Gordy Wren became (in 1948) the first person ever to qualify for all four Olympic skiing events. Aspen child star Jimmie Huega went on to win an Olympic bronze medal in 1964. Many non-native champs have made their homes in Colorado: head coach for the U.S. Alpine Team, Bob Beattie; college stars "Spider" Sabich and Mike Gallagher; world champions Stein Eriksen, Andrea Mead Lawrence, Billy Kidd, and Willy Schaeffler.

Colorado Ski Country USA

## COLORADO SKI COUNTRY USA

Mouthpiece of the Colorado ski industry, CSCUSA began in 1964, as a liaison between the resorts and the government, regulatory agencies, media, the travel industry, and the public. Its magazine-format annual Consumer Guide offers one-stop shopping for comparative information on each of Colorado's commercial ski areas. CSCUSA is comprised of four departments:

*MARKETING* - produces the Consumer Guide, organizes ski weeks and other promotional campaigns. Acts as liaison to the Colorado Tourism Board, and coordinates corporate sponsorship agreements.

*PUBLIC RELATIONS* - Handles requests for information from individual consumers and major media, disseminates press kits, photos, and informational brochures. Provides a 24-hour snow report via phone: (303) 831-SNOW.

*GOVERNMENTAL AFFAIRS* - Lobbies for and monitors legislation at state and federal levels that affects the ski industry, and deals with regulatory agencies.

*AREA OPERATIONS*- Works with the resorts on issues such as lift maintenance and safety, snowmaking, food service, personnel (in ski industry management positions), collects and analyzes data on the industry.

Aspen Skiing Co.

# ASPEN MOUNTAIN

ASPEN--the name is synonymous with skiing, and Aspen Mountain is the original ski area in the Aspen complex. First called Ajax, the mountain opened in 1947, having been discovered by Elizabeth Paepcke and her husband Walter, president of the Container Corporation of America. The ski area helped to turn Aspen from a ghost town into a major national cultural and recreational resort, home of the Aspen Music Festival and the Aspen Institute. Most of the big names in skiing have had an influence on Aspen's development, including Fred Iselin, Dick Durrance, Darcey Brown and Friedl Pfeifer.

Today, Apsen Mountain boasts the greatest vertical rise, single-stage gondola in the world. The six-passenger *Silver Queen* carries skiers from Aspen's base of 7,945 feet up a 3,267 vertical rise to the summit at 11,212. In addition, there are three quads, and five double chairs. More than 70 trails on 625 acres lead down 23 miles of runs, the longest of which is three miles. The mix of trail difficulty is nice: about a third are beginning runs, a third intermediate, and just under a third for advanced skiers. All the usual skier services can be found at the area.

Aspen Skiing Co.

## BUTTERMILK

When John Denver wrote *Aspenglow*, the ambiance typical of Buttermilk Mountain likely helped to inspire him. Buttermilk is the "family mountain" of the Aspen complex. Nearly 75% of its trails are for beginning and intermediate skiers, making it a good area for groups with a variety of abilities. Because of the challenging terrain of early Ajax (Aspen) Mountain, European ski champ Friedl Pfeifer developed Buttermilk in the 1960s, for those seeking a slightly smaller challenge.

Buttermilk's longest run is three miles, from a peak elevation of 9,900 feet. Its base elevation of 7,870 gives it a vertical drop of 2,030 feet. Six double chairs can carry 6,297 skiers per hour up the mountain. From the top, 45 trails descend over 402 acres--more than 20 miles of runs! If that's not enough, you can purchase a four-area ticket, good at Aspen Mountain, Aspen Highlands, and Snowmass. In 1987, Vic Braden, who pioneered tennis instruction, and is considered one of the finest sports teachers in America, opened the Vic Braden Aspen College of Skiing. Buttermilk is not *all* buttermilk, though. On the Tiehack side of the mountain are expert runs, often with deep powder, where world class competition is held on the "Racer's Edge."

Snowmass Resort Assoc.

# SNOWMASS

Managed by the Aspen Ski Corp., with Aspen Mountain and Buttermilk, Snowmass is 12 miles west of town. Lift tickets among the Aspen areas are interchangeable. Snowmass opened in 1967, as Snowmass-at-Aspen to distinguish it from the nearby older town of Snowmass.

The area offers 1,560 acres of skiable terrain; 90 runs on 55 miles of trails. The longest run is a wonderful 3.7 miles. Only 10% of Snowmass' trails are for beginners, 62% for intermediates, and 28% for advanced and expert skiers. Ten double chairs, two quads and two triple chairs carry 18,675 skiers per hour up the mountain. Snowmass' anticipated yearly snowfall is 300 inches on the 11,775-foot summit. Base elevation is 8,220, for a vertical drop of 3,555 feet.

The Snowmass Ski School is staffed by more than 250 instructors. There are children's programs, women's clinics, a B.O.L.D. program for blind and handicapped skiers, and special naturalist-guided snowshoe tours. The world's largest full-time working dog sled kennel, the famous Krabloonlik, is nearby. More than 95% of the lodges at Snowmass are on the mountain, and Snowmass Village boasts the largest conference facility in the Rocky Mountains.

Aspen Highlands Ski Corp.

## ASPEN HIGHLANDS

Advertising the longest vertical drop in Colorado, 3,800 feet, Aspen Highlands stands as an independent corporation amid the nearby giant, Aspen Ski Corp. From the summit of 11,800 feet to the base of 8,000, Aspen Highlands offers 450 acres of skiing on 66 trails, the longest being 3-1/2 miles. Lift capacity is 10,000 skiers per hour. Although it receives 300 inches of natural snow a year, Aspen Highlands does make snow on its lower runs.

The area was a post-war baby boomer, founded by Fred Iselin of Sun Valley fame. With the breathtaking Maroon Bells rising as a backdrop, The Highlands offers "just the thrills; not the frills," yet provides all the services that a serious skier needs. There is a complete ski school and nursery school, NASTAR, weekly freestyle competition, self-timed racing, video taping, and a personal ski evaluation.

While it is not a part of Aspen Ski Corp., Highlands does participate in a "four mountain ticket" plan which also affords skiers an opportunity to ski at Buttermilk, Aspen, and Snowmass. Located three miles southwest of Aspen, the Highlands is connected to town by a free shuttle bus that runs every 15 minutes.

David Lokey, Vail

# VAIL/BEAVER CREEK

Mecca of skiers world-wide, but particularly Texas skiers, is chic, unique Vail. From its conception in 1954, Vail has been blessed with enthusiastic investors and extremely good publicity, particularly when Gerald Ford made it his western White House. The opening of the Eisenhower Tunnel in 1973, made Vail much more accessible from Denver, 100 miles to the east.

Today Vail is touted as the largest single mountain ski complex in Colorado. Its capacity of 28,800 persons per hour is made possible by a high-speed enclosed quad chair lift, three other non-enclosed express quad chairs, a gondola, three triple chairs, nine doubles and a child's poma lift. The developed side of the mountain has a total of 92 trails, equally divided from beginner to advanced. On the undeveloped side of the mountain are the famous "Back Bowls" for expert skiers, rich (most years) in deep, fresh powder.

Vail's longest run is three-mile Riva Ridge, named in memory of the Tenth Mountain Division's Italian encounter. From its base at 8,150 feet, it rises to 11,250, a vertical drop of 3,100. Complete with every skier service, Vail averages 300-350 inches of snow a year, and claims sunshine on 70% of its skiing days.

Beaver Creek Resort

When the prospect of Colorado's hosting the 1976 Winter Olympics died, development of Beaver Creek, just 10 miles from Vail in nearby Avon, was severely delayed. Promoters had hoped to capitalize on the Olympics to ensure development of Beaver Creek, but environmentalists had other ideas. The tenacity of Vail's Robert Park to prevail against the governor, a Senator, the U.S. Forest Service and 51 governmental stipulations, made the opening of Beaver Creek a reality during the 1980-81 season.

One of the last major ski areas to be built in the U.S., Beaver Creek sits on 5,600 acres in the White River National Forest. With a percentage of its runs slightly weighted to intermediate and advanced skiers, Beaver Creek maintains 49 trails. Its longest is Centennial, a 2-3/4 mile run. The area's variety of double, triple and quad chair lifts service 15,639 skiers per hour.

The Vail and Beaver Creek ski schools have a total of 600 instructors, 135 of whom specialize in teaching children. There are lessons for toddlers, and special mountains at each area for children: Peanut Peak at Vail and Buckaroo Bowl at Beaver Creek. Vail has hosted some of the most prestigious World Cup races, and the 1989 World Alpine Ski Championships will be held at Beaver Creek.

Jeff Andrew, Keystone

# KEYSTONE

It was 1942 when forestry professor Max Dercum moved his family to a remote ranch near today's Keystone resort. Named the Ski Tip Ranch for the door latches made of guest's broken ski parts, Max, Edna and associates went on to found Arapahoe Basin in 1946. A Basin (as it was known through some of its existence) and the Ski Tip Lodge were subsequently acquired by Keystone in 1984. Today, Arapahoe Basin is one of three areas that comprise the Keystone resort, along with Keystone Mt. and North Peak.

It's an area of superlatives. Arapahoe Basin is the highest lift-served area in North America; more than half its terrain is above timberline. Base elevation is 10,780, summit 12,450. This is a late-season area, June skiing being not uncommon. Arapahoe Basin's 22 trails are served by one triple and four double chair lifts. Only 10% of its slopes are rated for beginners; 90% for intermediate to advanced skiers. The area receives 360 inches of snow per year.

Keystone Mt. is the largest single mountain night ski operation in the U.S. The enclosed Skyway Gondola shuttles skiers to the top of the 13 trails on 200 lighted acres. There are 39 trails on this mountain, the longest

Jeff Andrew, Keystone

three miles. In addition to the gondola, this mountain is served by eight double chair lifts, one triple and two surface lifts, accommodating 13,400 skiers per hour. Keystone Mt. advertises 65% of its trails for intermediates, 20% for beginners and 15% for advanced. At North Peak, the third part of the complex, 78% of the trails are for advanced skiers, and 22% for intermediate. None are recommended for beginners.

The prestigious Mahre Training Centers are a service of Keystone. Here, any age or ability skier can learn special techniques focusing on balance and control, developed by the U.S. Ski Team Director and the Mahres. Video taping gives instant feedback on one's progress. A complete resort with all the amenities and adjunct recreational programs, Keystone also has the largest maintained ice facility in the country. At the Keystone Resort, children 12 and under stay free. Keystone Ranch, on the golf course, features six-course gourmet dinners. The 60-year-old ranch house was built around a stone fireplace--a wedding gift to the original owners.

The opening of the Keystone resort in 1970 was the culmination of a lifetime dream for the Dercums. And to recount the days since the one-room Ski Tip Ranch, Edna subsequently authored *It's Easy Edna, It's Downhill all the Way.*

Jeff Andrew, Copper Mtn.

# Copper Mountain

Just east of Vail Pass, where Colorado Hwy. 91 meets I-70, 75 miles west of Denver, is Copper Mountain, considered by many to be one of the top 10 ski resorts in the country. Copper is a year-round resort. The Copper Creek Golf Course (7,000 yards, par 70) is the highest altitude championship course in America. There are cycling camps, art festivals, concerts, pack trips, jeep tours to ghost towns, hiking, horseback riding and a kids fishing pond--just for starters! Copper's Racquet and Athletic Club offers another complete array of facilities. Copper Mountain is a self-sufficient community, with most municipal services, a car rental and travel agency.

It wasn't always like this... Back when Colorado was in the running for the 1976 Winter Olympics, Copper Mountain was proposed by the Forest Service as a sight for the games, despite the fact that there were no tows erected there at the time. The prospect of Colorado as a host died, but the prospect of Copper did not. An executive at Vail, lured by this pristine land west of Dillon, joined forces with the headmaster of a private school in Denver, secured additional backing from the McCormick family of farm equipment fame, to open in

Jeff Andrew, Copper Mtn.

1973. Ultimately, Apex Petroleum purchased the resort, and its success is unquestioned. Copper is now an official training site for the U.S. Ski Team.

Copper Mountain is 9,600 feet at the base, 12,360 at the summit. Situated on 1,180 skiable acres, it has nine double chairs, six triples, and one quad in addition to four surface lifts to accommodate skiers. Of its 75 miles of trails, 35% are for advanced skiers, 40% for intermediate, and 25% for beginners. The longest run is 2.8 miles. With an annual snowfall of 255 inches per year, you wouldn't think Copper would need much snowmaking equipment, but it does provide it on 200 acres of the development. There is also a 25 km. maintained cross-country track.

*Ski Magazine* recently rated Copper Mountain's youth programs as second in the country. Programs include the Belly Button Babies for 2 mos. to 2 years, the Belly Button Bakery for 2-4 year-olds, the Junior Ranch for 4-6 year-olds, complete with its own lift, and the Senior Ranch for ages 7-12. There are racing workshops, a self-timed trail, personalized video analysis, and an adult ski school with special women's skiing seminars. If Copper Mountain sounds strictly like a destination resort, consider the "Copper Choppers," a ski program for kids 8-18, with bus service to Copper from nine locations in metro Denver.

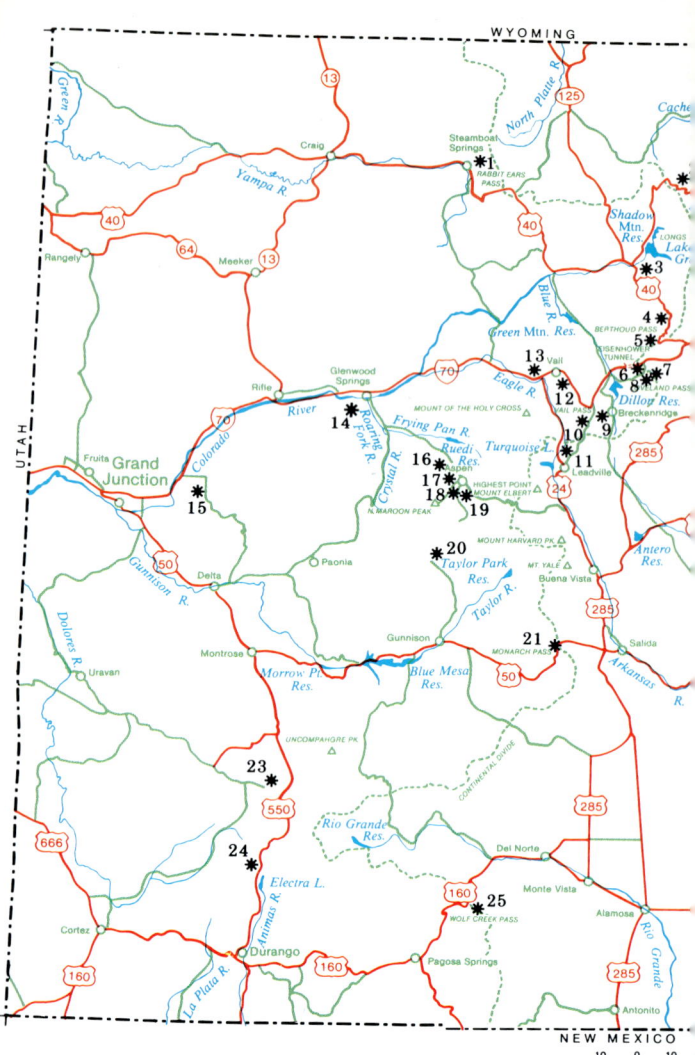

# SKI AREA DIRECTORY

1. Steamboat
2. Ski Estes Park
3. Silver Creek
4. Winter Park
5. Berthoud
6. Loveland
7. Arapahoe Basin
8. Keystone
9. Breckenridge
10. Copper Mountain
11. Ski Cooper
12. Vail

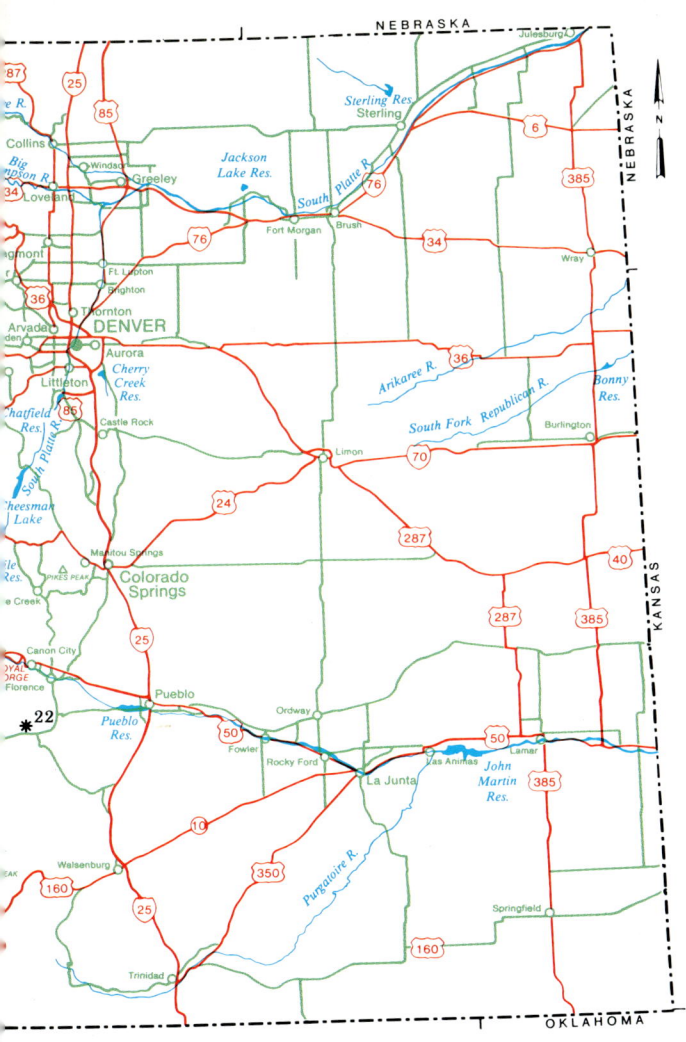

13. Beaver Creek
14. Ski Sunlight
15. Powderhorn
16. Snowmass
17. Buttermilk
18. Aspen Highlands
19. Aspen Mountain
20. Crested Butte
21. Monarch
22. Conquistador
23. Telluride
24. Purgatory
25. Wolf Creek

Carl Scofield, Breckenridge Ski Area

# BRECKENRIDGE

Many of Colorado's ghost towns have remained just that. Breckenridge was a boom town from the time the first gold was turned in 1859. By the 1940s, though, the boom had played out and Breckenridge seemed destined for the ghost town roster. But with the opening of the ski area in 1961, the town's economy began an upward swing, and now this Summit County town can boast of being the oldest continually occupied community on Colorado's Western Slope. The 128-year-old Victorian town includes Colorado's largest National Historic District--354 buildings.

Breckenridge Ski Area is actually three independent mountains, all connected by lifts and trails. Peak 8 rises to an elevation of 12,213 feet, a vertical rise of more than 2,500 feet. Peaks 9 and 10 are slightly lower. If you're an experienced skier, Peak 10 is your cup of tea. Only 2% of its trails are rated "easiest," while 67% are rated "expert." It is serviced by only one lift, but that is a quad "super chair." Peak 8 also rates more than half of its trails for expert skiers. It has seven lifts--five double chairs, one quad and one surface lift--to carry skiers to the top of 857 skiable acres. For those of us who don't want quite that challenge, Peak 9 is the place to be. There, 43% of the trails are rated "easiest" and

Carl Scofield, Breckenridge Ski Area   SNOWBOARDING

46% "intermediate." Four double chairs, one triple and one quad serve this mountain. Combined, Breckenridge lifts can move 22,050 skiers per hour uphill.

Virtually every service is available to the skier at Breckenridge. Peak 8 provides a nursery and children's programs. A 180-instructor ski school offers every type of lesson from beginning level to racing, powder, freestyle, and mogul skiing, as well as telemark and snowboarding instruction. There is a handicapped ski program, NASTAR and self-timed race courses, and free tours of the mountains. To capture yourself on film, the area offers both video and still photographers. Heli-skiing provides the more adventurous with a helicopter transport to carry them into the back country for some deep powder skiing in pristine areas. There are also 45 kilometers of groomed cross-country trails in the area.

Breckenridge, 85 miles west of Denver, offers luxury condos, townhomes, private houses, hotels, bed & breakfast inns and dorm rooms. In town are an array of restaurants and other diversions. In or near Breckenridge, you can ice skate, play miniature golf, go snow mobiling, dog sledding, sleigh riding, snowcatting, or swimming. There is an historical tour of the area, a theater and art galleries.

Winter Park                     HANDICAPPED SKI PROGRAM

## WINTER PARK

**P**art of the Denver Mountain Parks system, and therefore administered by the City of Denver, Winter Park is actually 67 miles northwest of the city. Two areas, Winter Park and Mary Jane, comprise the development, located at the west portal of the Moffat Tunnel. Nearing its golden anniversary, Winter Park is one of the state's largest areas, with 90 designated trails, 18 chair lifts (three triples and three quads) to accommodate more than 24,000 skiers per hour. Mary Jane, catering to intermediate and advanced skiers, opened in 1975.   About as high as you can get at Winter Park is 11,220 feet, which allows you a vertical drop of 2,200 feet to the approximate base altitude of 9,000 feet. The longest run at the area is the one connecting Mary Jane to Winter Park, a distance of 2-1/2 miles. The complex does make snow, but Mother Nature provides an average of 250 inches per season at Winter Park and 364 inches at Mary Jane.

Few skier services are overlooked at Winter Park. There is a nursery complete with children's ski school. NASTAR races are held every day. There are clinics on competition, waxing, equipment maintenance as well as a ski school complete in every function for beginning to expert skiers. To improve your racing performance, the

Winter Park                      WEST PORTAL, MOFFAT TUNNEL

area offers *Coca-Cola Ski Time,* a coin-operated race course which displays a skier's time at the end of the run. For the non-alpine skier, there is cross-country skiing, snowmobiling, ice skating, mountain tours, sleigh rides, tubing, ice fishing, and more.

Famous world-wide for its handicapped ski program, Winter Park preaches a philosophy of "rehabilitation through recreation." The program was launched in 1970 by Hal O'Leary, who volunteered to teach 23 handicapped children from Children's Hospital in Denver. It is now the largest in the world, with 75 specially trained instructors who challenge 15,000 children per year. Assisting these special instructors are more than 700 volunteers, working with 42 different kinds of disabilities, from amputation to visual impairment. A summer program originated in 1977 offers mountain climbing, river rafting, and other sports.

You can reach Winter Park by bus or car. But a more romantic form of transportation is the Winter Park Ski Train, operated by the Denver & Rio Grande Railroad since shortly after the opening of the Moffat Tunnel. Until 1933, the Berthoud Pass highway was closed in the winter, so the train was a necessity to fledgling Winter Park. It has continually gained favor, both for convenience and camaraderie.

Steamboat Ski Corp.

# STEAMBOAT

WERNER--the name is everywhere in Steamboat. The late Buddy Werner, Steamboat's native son who won accolades at the 1956, 1960 and 1964 winter Olympics, became a martyred hero when he was killed in an avalanche in the Swiss Alps following Olympic competition in '64. In Buddy's honor, the town renamed nearby Storm Mountain, Mount Werner, and a number of other landmarks carry his name as well. The original Storm Mountain had opened for skiing in 1962, with one lift and an A-frame warming hut. The challenging headwall was serviced by one poma lift. Skiing has been a way of life in Steamboat Springs since 1916, when the first jump was built on what would later become Howelsen Hill. In 1936, the high school band began marching on skis. (By 1960, a system of rollers was developed for the skis, so the band could perform in warmer climates!) Some of the major names in skiing have been associated with Steamboat Springs.

Today, the area consists of 2,500 acres, 1,400 of them groomed, and is comprised of four major peaks. Its vertical drop is the second longest in Colorado: 3,600 feet from the summit of 10,500 to the base of 6,900. There are 100 trails, the longest three miles. Slightly more than half of the trails are for intermediate

Steamboat Ski Corp.

skiers; 31% for advanced and 15% for beginners. The 20 lifts include nine double chairs, seven triples, one quad and the gondola, accommodating 28,730 skiers per hour. Snowfall averages 325-350 inches per year.

Vermont Olympic champion Billy Kidd, now Steamboat's director of skiing, also directs the Billy Kidd Racing Camps, is head ski coach for the Special Olympics, and advisor for the President's Council on Physical Fitness and Sports. Kidd and Jimmie Heuga were the first American men to win Olympic medals in skiing. In support of Heuga, who now suffers from MS, Kidd has become involved in MS fund raising campaigns.

Steamboat Springs offers NASTAR races daily (except Mondays) and the Marlboro Ski Challenge, a coin operated race course. The ski school is staffed by 200 certified alpine instructors, competent in telemarking, mogul skiing, racing, teaching the handicapped, and video analysis. There are seven certified Nordic instructors. In downtown Steamboat, home of some of Colorado's first winter carnivals, there are chariot races, hydrotubing, powder cat skiing, hot air ballooning, ice skating, and sleigh rides. This in addition to the natural phenomenon that gave the town its name: hot springs, one of which the old-timers determined, sounded like the chugging of a river steamer's engine!

Stanley Zamonski — EARLY '50s SKI SCHOOL

## LOVELAND

The most accessible major ski area from Denver, Loveland is located approximately 50 miles west of the metro area on I-70, just before the Eisenhower Tunnel. While overnight accommodations are not available directly on the premises, the delightful restored Victorian silver mining area of Georgetown offers nearly every traveler service. Perched at the eastern foot of Loveland Pass, this area records some of the highest annual snowfalls in Colorado.

Loveland Pass is named for W.A.H. Loveland, Colorado transportation pioneer. Thwarted in his attempt to build a railroad over the Continental Divide, Loveland constructed his "High Line Wagon Road" over the pass, to transport the mineral wealth out of the mountains beyond. Since the 1920s, the more daring and accomplished have attempted to ski 11,992-foot Loveland Pass, which is now traversed by U.S. Highway 6. In good weather, this route is a beautiful 12-mile drive between Loveland Ski Area at the eastern base of the pass, and Arapahoe Basin at the western base.

The enthusiasm of early skiers for Loveland Pass, led to the development of ski runs and the opening of Loveland Basin as a ski area in the 1930s. Colorado suffered its first accident-related recreational skiing

Loveland Ski Area

casualty on Loveland Pass, May 21, 1939, when Berrien Hughes (for whom Hughes run at Winter Park is named) hit a rock. Pete Seibert, a Tenth Mountain Division veteran, managed Loveland Basin in the '50s, and later helped found Vail.

Eight lifts--four double chairs, two triples, a beginner's chair lift and a poma service the area. Loveland Valley is connected to the main mountain, Loveland Basin, by a double chair. The summit of Loveland Basin, at 12,240, is well above timberline. Base elevation is 10,800. There are 640 skiable acres at Loveland, 130 serviced by snowmaking equipment which often makes Loveland one of the first areas to open for the season. At the area proper, there are rental and repair shops, restaurants and child care facilities.

When Loveland found itself curiously sprawled around the eastern approach to the Eisenhower Tunnel, promoters decided, "Hey, there's lots of great terrain on the North Side and we aren't going to let a little ol' interstate keep you away from it." So at the bottom of the northern mountain, to avoid the nasty problem of having to traverse I-70 on skis, Loveland constructed a tunnel which funnels skiers under the highway and back to the lift entrances again!

# CRESTED BUTTE

TELEMARK SKI CAPITAL OF THE WORLD! That's how Crested Butte advertises itself. This increasingly popular Norwegian ski technique (often used for control and stability down long, straight runs) that emphasizes shifting the weight forward on the outside ski in a turn and guiding its tip gradually inward. Cross-country and telemark are big attractions at Crested Butte, in addition to its standard downhill facilities. Located approximately 25 miles north of Gunnison, the area averages 300 inches of snow from October to April. There are runs for all abilities, with emphasis on the intermediate skier. For the over-50 crowd, Crested Butte Ski School offers a class called Vintage Skiers.

In 1974, the entire town of Crested Butte was designated a National Historic District. The Ute Indians had used it as a summer hunting grounds before the first miners arrived for the gold and silver boom. Snow has not always been a blessing in this region. It is said that these early miners were forced to construct two-story outhouses for winter use! The discovery of coal in the 1880s boosted the sagging gold and silver economy. By 1952, however, even coal could not support the residents, and the town might have disappeared, but for the development of the ski area in 1963.

# SKI ESTES PARK

Formerly Hidden Valley, this area is within the boundaries of Rocky Mountain National Park via Trail Ridge Road (U.S. 36). As the area became more popular in the late '50s, road crews were persuaded to keep a portion of Trail Ridge open for access. Rates here are some of the lowest in the state, yet half of its runs are rated "most difficult;" 30 % are intermediate and 20 % for beginners. The longest run is 1.5 miles. From a summit elevation of 11,500 feet, runs drop 2,000 feet to the base. Two T-bars and two poma lifts service the area, with a shuttle bus to the upper mountain. Just 10 miles west of Estes Park, the area advertises itself as "an affordable alternative."

Robert Hagan, Telluride Ski Resort

# TELLURIDE

Installation of the longest high speed chair lift in the world (1,750 vertical feet in 11 minutes) has opened a new mountain at Telluride--Sunshine Peak for beginning and intermediate skiers. Its location in the Uncompahgre National Forest of southwestern Colorado's rugged San Juan Mountains would make you think that Telluride was no place for a beginning skier, but 14% of its slopes are for this ability, and 54% for intermediate skiers. Only the Front Face area of the mountain is for experts. This area has a steep vertical drop with deep powder and mogul chutes. There are 45 trails on 735 skiable acres, serviced by a quad chair lift, six double, two triple chairs, and one poma lift. The area averages 300 inches of snow per year.

Today, Telluride is easily accessible by air, but not so in the early days when miners headed there for silver. One disgruntled train passenger, huddled beside a poorly burning wood stove in the back of the passenger section, was overheard cursing (either the town or the transportation) *"To-Hell-You-Ride."* This, however, was not how the town got its name. The origin is in the element Tellurium, which often is found attached to silver in its natural state.

# Wolf Creek

Where do you go to find the most snow in Colorado? Country singer C.W. McCall told you in his hit song: *Wolf Creek Pass, way up on the Great Divide.* There, of an average winter, the ski area gets a whopping 465 inches of snow! Wolf Creek is truly a haven for deep powder enthusiasts, offering back country tours in addition to its downhill trails. The ski area is located on the pass, with a base elevation of 10,650, the summit at 11,775, for a vertical rise of 1,125 feet. High altitude sun is always a threat to skin and eyes, but at this altitude, sunglasses and sunscreen are a *must*.

There are slopes for all abilities at Wolf Creek, a well-balanced mix of beginning, intermediate and advanced trails. The longest, pleasantly named Tranquility, is 1.6 miles. Wolf Creek can accommodate 3,680 skiers per hour on its triple and double chairs and pomas. While no lodging is available right at the area, both sides of the pass offer a variety of overnight spots. Pagosa Springs is approximately 25 miles to the south; Durango a total of 75 south and west. Without the glitter of the giant resorts, Wolf Creek has, nevertheless, served Colorado skiers consistently since the days before World War II.

# Berthoud

Colorado's first ski area opened in February, 1937, and is still operating today. Before 1932, Berthoud Pass was closed in the winter, but from 1932 until the area opened in 1937, skiers would be driven to the top of the pass and ski down trails to the bottom. The first ski lift in the state was at Berthoud, an 848-foot rope tow powered by a $300 Ford V-8 engine. Just 12 years later, in October of 1939, Berthoud Ski Area installed a double chair lift, the first in North America, and, to the best of the area's knowledge, the first in the world.

That chair lift is still carrying skiers up the mountain today, along with a T-Bar. At the top is the highest base lodge in North America, perched on the Continental Divide at 11,314 feet. During the 1982-83 season, Berthoud received its record snowfall: 653 inches in one year!

Schweikle, Purgatory Resort           THE ALPINE SLIDE

# PURGATORY

Durango, Queen City of southwestern Colorado, offers skiing just 25 miles north at Purgatory. Purgatory, said the early Spanish explorers, was where all lost souls were transported. (Nearby is the Rio de Las Animas--"lost souls" in Spanish.) The area opened in 1967, the brainchild of Forest Service weatherman Chet Anderson. Subsequently, a former head of Vail Associates managed the area, bringing to it much of the knowledge that had made Vail a success. The opening of the Tamarron Resort, between Durango and Purgatory, was also a boost to the area. Today, Purgatory has developed 630 skiable acres, half of which are intermediate trails. There is a 2,022 foot vertical drop from the 10,822-foot summit. Five double chairs and four triples serve the area, which receives an annual snowfall of 300 inches.

Purgatory's handicapped ski program is considered one of the industry's most successful. In addition to its standard skier amenities, among them the Village Resort with banquet facilities, Purgatory has installed an Alpine Slide for summer visitors. The Durango/Silverton Narrow Gauge Steam Train also runs daily in the summer for a delightful day-trip into history.

# Silver Creek

Silver Creek is, first and foremost, a resort and convention center, located 15 miles north of Winter Park, near Granby. Of the newer areas which have opened in the midst of strict environmental regulations and astronomical construction costs, Silver Creek has been one of the few to prosper. Skiing is only one of the many activities available to guests year-round at Silver Creek--the biggest ski resort on private land in the state. Convention facilities can accommodate some of the largest meetings in the Rocky Mountain region. Silver Creek offers five lifts on 200 skiable acres, with approximately half of the runs geared to intermediate skiers. Elevation at the summit is 9,202 feet. An adjacent Nordic center provides a 25-km cross-country track for beginning through advanced skiers, or you may wish to enhance your ski vacation with some ice skating and sleigh rides. Considering the number of services available at the area, Silver Creek's prices are most reasonable, particularly for groups.

# Ski Cooper

Terrain that served as a training ground for the Tenth Mountain Division's crack ski troops in World War II, is now available to the public at Ski Cooper. Tucked high in the Colorado Rockies, 10 miles north of Leadville on Tennessee Pass is the original Camp Hale area, opened in 1942. When the military developed its primary run on Cooper Hill, it also erected what was, at that time, the world's longest T-bar lift. The army took over Cooper Hill again during the Korean War.

Leadville is one of highest towns in the state, so Ski Cooper is naturally a high altitude area--10,500 feet at the base and 11,700 at the summit. It snows there too--an average of 250 inches per year. Today, a triple and double chair, a T-bar and a poma lift can accommodate nearly 3,400 skiers per hour. Ski Cooper offers all the amenities, from ski school to nursery to rental shop, right at the area. For non-skiers, there are dog sled races at Cooper, or you may find yourself traveling to nearby Leadville to retrace the Tabors' saga and the area's early mining history.

Ski Sunlight

# SKI SUNLIGHT

Its location just ten miles southwest of Glenwood Springs, home of the world's largest hot springs pool, makes Sunlight an attractive place for a ski vacation. Glenwood was a health spa and tourist attraction even before Theodore Roosevelt stayed at the Hotel Colorado on his unproductive hunting expedition. (It was a chambermaid there, remember, who felt so sorry for Roosevelt that she made him a stuffed animal--the world's original Teddy Bear.)

Sunlight offers 30 runs, half of which are on intermediate terrain. Colorado Governor John Vanderhoof had originally seen development possibilities in a mountain he called Holiday Hill. With the financing of Chicago artist John Kiggs, Sunlight opened officially in 1966. Its summit elevation is 9,895 feet and the longest run is 2-1/2 miles. At the top of the mountain, the annual snowfall averages 260 inches. Sunlight is serviced by two double chair lifts and a surface lift. It offers a professional ski school, a coin operated dual race course at the Dotsero Race Arena, and will arrange races for groups upon request. Of importance to skiing families: children five and under ski free at Sunlight; day care and accommodations available.

Nathan Bilow, Monarch Ski Resort

# Monarch

When Monarch opened in 1939, lift tickets were 25 cents per day; a season's pass $1.00. Sound unbelievable? Consider the facilities: one ski run and a rope tow! The area was built as a WPA project of the Civilian Conservation Corps in 1933, and has been open annually since then. As originally conceived, it was a day area for residents of Salida. The old rope tow served the area well until 1959, when Monarch modernized with a T-bar. A year later, the first chair lift went in, made of parts from west Texas oil fields, the towers constructed from well casings and old oil derricks. By 1978, the area had added another chair.

Today, Monarch's 50 trails are serviced by four double chair lifts and a gondola. Located on the Continental Divide near the summit of Monarch Pass, the area has a base elevation of 10,800 feet, and a summit height of 11,800 feet. About half of its trails are for intermediate skiers, the remaining half divided evenly between beginner and advanced. Over 300 inches of snow falls here each year. Among its other services, Monarch offers 3-day Women's Ski Seminars, designed and taught by women instructors. Intermediate or better skiers can have a Personal Skiing Analysis at no charge.

Conquistador, Raw Studios Photography

## Conquistador

From Colorado Springs, Pueblo or Canon City, an ideal day area is Conquistador, five miles west of Westcliffe, in the Sangre de Cristo mountains. Legend has it that a group of Spanish explorers who had come north looking for gold, were prospecting in the area one fall afternoon when they were attacked by Indians. One of the men, mortally wounded by an arrow, looked up to see the sun shining through the bright red autumn leaves. *"Sangre de Cristo,"* (Blood of Christ) he cried out, and the mountain range was thus named.

Conquistador is serviced by a triple and double chair lift, and two pony tows. Of its 12 trails, 30% are for beginners and 55% for intermediate skiers. Conquistador claims the largest snowmaking gun in the world; however, its natural snow averages 350 inches at the 10,100 summit, 200 inches at the base. In addition to its ski school of 55 instructors, Conquistador offers a Little Critters program for 3-5 year olds, day care service, a coin operated racing system and cross country programs. Opened in 1982, the area makes a nice alternative to the more expensive developments. Here, an all-day lift ticket is in the $15 range for adults, $9.00 for children. Senior citizens ski free!

Powderhorn Ski Resort

# POWDERHORN

An easy 35-mile drive from Grand Junction, air hub of western Colorado, Powderhorn is located in the Grand Mesa National Forest. As early as the 1920s, skiers were braving it off the edge of Grand Mesa, the world's largest flat-topped mountain. Today's Powderhorn area is on the north rim of the mesa. In 1966, Bob Sayer, a veteran of Colorado's famed Tenth Mountain Division of World War II days, undertook development of the area. Its first year, 21,000 skiers purchased tickets, hardly enough for the area to thrive. But with the help of outside investors, the area had soon doubled its ticket sales. In 1986, Dallas businessman Jim Scott purchased Powderhorn, beginning a $5-million improvement and construction plan. An additional $18-million is scheduled for further development in the immediate future.

Currently, Powderhorn has four lifts on 225 skiable acres. Snowmaking equipment is used on 50 acres. The base elevation is 8,200 feet, and the summit 9,850. More than 200 inches of extra-light snow falls here annually, giving Powderhorn some of the best powder skiing in the west. What it may currently lack in size, Powderhorn makes up for in ambiance.

Colorado Ski Museum — BERTHOUD PASS SKI AREA, 1946

# COLORADO SKI MUSEUM

Founded in 1976 to preserve the history of skiing in Colorado, this delightful museum is located in the heart of ski country, between Vail and Lionshead. Six galleries display artifacts, photos, equipment and clothing from the early days of skiing. Exhibits feature military skiing and the Tenth Mountain Division; Presidential skiing; cross-country; the evolution of ski equipment; the role of the U.S. Forest Service in the development of ski areas. The museum's theater shows historical films and offers multi-image presentations with such intriguing titles as *Skinny Skiing, From Showshoes to Slalom,* and the *Aspen Album.*

Another regular exhibit is the Colorado Ski Hall of Fame. Instituted in 1977 to honor men and women who have contributed to skiing in Colorado, the Hall of Fame is approaching 75 members. Included are such greats as Lowell Thomas, Willy Schaeffler, Buddy Werner, and Jimmie Heuga.

Museum and theater admission is free. Membership benefits include a ski museum pin, the newsletter, a discount on museum merchandise, invitations to and consultation privileges on ski-related functions. For information, write P.O. Box 1976; Vail, CO 81658.

# CROSS-COUNTRY

As the popularity of downhill skiing increased in the '60s and '70s, so did the crowds, the lift lines, and the commercialism. To many who skied for solace and solitude, the only recourse was the backcountry, and with that retreat came a resurgance in Nordic skiing. As more people became enthusiasts, trails were developed and maintained. The Colorado Cross Country Ski Association in Granby acts as a clearinghouse for information on the sport. There are many commercial cross country centers around the state, including:

*C Lazy U Ranch* - (Granby) 30 km of machined trails, supplemented by thousands of acres of backcountry skiing.
*Conejos Ranch Ski Touring Center* - (Antonito) 100 acres of marked trails with central accommodations.
*Frisco Cross Country Recreational Area* - 35 km of machined trails, with additional backcountry skiing.
*Paragon Guides* - (Vail) an experienced guide service which offers backcountry tours with a hut system.
*Peaceful Valley Ski Ranch* - (Lyons) 75 km of trails, with guides and lodging available.
*Snow Mountain Ranch* - (Winter Park) 50 km of trails, headquartered at YMCA of the Rockies; lodging available.
*Vista Verde Ski Ranch* - (Steamboat Springs) 20 km of maintained trails, with instruction, guides and lodging.

For those interested in non-commercial areas, a sampling of trailheads and access points:

*Aspen* - Hunter Creek Trail: follow South Mill north from town across the Roaring Fork River to a Y, taking the left branch to the next junction.
*Boulder Area* - Brainard Lake: north from Ward on Colo. 72, take Brainard Lake road on the left; East Portal: take dirt road west from Rollinsville to the east portal of the Moffat Tunnel.
*Colorado Springs Area* - Black Forest Park: Take Colo. 83 NE of town to Shoup Rd., and head east. Crags Campground: South on Colo. 67 from Divide to Rocky Mt. Mennonite Camp, then east.
*Denver Area* - Golden Gate Canyon: a state park, 15 miles NW of Golden off Colo. 93.
*Durango* - Junction Creek: Six miles north of town on Junction Creek Rd.; Hermosa Meadows: 10 mi. N of town on U.S. 550.
*Estes Park / Rocky Mountain National Park* - Wild Basin and Bear Lake areas very popular, but dozens of trail heads within the park. Check with Park Headquarters for maps and details. Guided tours also available; check with Chamber of Commerce (586-4431).
*Fort Collins* - Rawah Wilderness area: 75 miles west of Ft. Collins in Roosevelt National Forest near Medicine Bow Mountains.
*Georgetown* - Guanella Pass: Take Guanella Pass road south from town approximately 10 miles to the top of the pass.
*Glenwood Springs* - Flattops Wilderness Area 20 miles north of town off Colo. 244, just west of Glenwood.

Snowmass Resort Association

*Grand Junction* - Grand Mesa area, contact Mesa Lakes Resort.
*Gunnison* - In Gunnison Ntl. Forest; or Mill Creek: north on Colo. 135 to Ohio Creek Rd., north 9 mi to Mill Creek Rd.
*Idaho Springs* - Chicago Lakes: turn off Colo. 103 at Idaho Springs reservoir between Chicago Forks and Ponder Point.
*Leadville* - Tennessee Pass: NW of Leadville on U.S. 24 to summit of Tennessee Pass.

In addition to the previous Nordic centers, these downhill resorts maintain cross-country facilities:

*Aspen/Snowmass* - 75 km double track connect Snowmass and Aspen; one of largest XC areas in North America
*Beaver Creek* - 30 km of double set track
*Breckenridge* - 45 km of groomed, double-set trails one mile from Peak 8. Connects with The Whatley Ranch, three mi. north of town.
*Conquistador* - limited XC from base; many forest service trails
*Copper Mt.* - Telemarking lessons daily; 25 km of XC trails
*Crested Butte* - 13 km of groomed tracks; overnight tours; telemark and flattrack instruction
*Keystone* - 27 km of trails from the Dercum's famous Ski Tip Lodge; telemark and moonlight tours available
*Monarch* - offers Nordic and telemark programs
*Purgatory* - 15 km groomed trails; offers telemarking clinics
*Silver Creek* - 25 km of trails; Nordic, telemark instruction
*Steamboat* - 20 km of trails; instruction and tours
*Ski Cooper* - lessons & tours, day or night; 26 mi of trails
*Ski Sunlight* - cross-country center at base
*Telluride* - 10km and 20km trails through the San Juans
*Vail* - break your own trail from the summit of Golden Peak, one of the oldest XC centers in the U.S.
*Winter Park:* at *Ski Idlewild* - 30 mi of trails; (see also Snow Mountain Ranch, above)

# Names & Numbers

**APSEN HIGHLANDS SKIING CORPORATION**
P.O. Box T;   Aspen, CO 81612       (303) 925-5300
**ASPEN SKIING COMPANY**
P.O. Box 1248; 117 Aspen Airport Business Center
Aspen, CO 81612       (303) 925-1220
**BEAVER CREEK**
P.O. Box 915;   Avon, CO 81620
(303) 949-5750       (1-800) 525-2257
**BRECKENRIDGE SKI AREA**
P.O. Box 1058;   1599 Summit Co. Rd. 3
Breckenridge, CO 80424       (303) 453-2368
**C LAZY U RANCH**
P.O. Box 378;   Granby, CO 80446   (303) 887-3344
**COLORADO CROSS COUNTRY SKI ASSOC.**
P.O. Box 1407;   Granby, CO 80446   (303) 887-3457
**COLORADO SKI COUNTRY USA**
1410 Grant St.;   Denver, CO 80203   (303) 837-0793
**COLORADO SKI MUSEUM**
P.O. Box 1976;   Vail, CO 81658   (303) 476-1876
**CONEJOS RANCH SKI TOURING CENTER**
Colo. Hwy. 17;   Antonito, CO 81120
(303) 376-5623
**CONQUISTADOR SKI RESORT**
P.O. Box 347;   Westcliffe, CO 81252   (303) 783-9206
**COPPER MOUNTAIN RESORT**
P.O. Box 3001;   Copper Mountain, CO 80443
(303) 968-2882
**CRESTED BUTTE SKI AREA**
P.O. Box 1288;   Crested Butte, CO 81224
(303) 349-2222
**FRISCO CROSS COUNTRY RECREATION AREA**
P.O. Box 207;   Frisco, CO 80443
(303) 668-5276; Toll free from Denver area: 893-1855
**KEYSTONE RESORT**
P.O. Box 38;   Keystone, CO 80435
(1-800) 222-0188;   (303) 468-2316
**LOVELAND SKI AREA**
P.O. Box 899;   Georgetown, CO 80444
(303) 569-2288   Toll free from Denver area: 571-5580
**MONARCH SKI RESORT**
Garfield, CO 81227;   (303) 539-2581
**PARAGON GUIDES**
P.O. Box 130; Vail, CO 81658;   (303) 949-5682

**PEACEFUL VALLEY SKI RANCH**
Star Route, Lyons, CO 80540; (303) 747-2881
Toll free from Denver area: 440-9632
**POWDERHORN SKI RESORT**
744 Horizon Drive; Grand Junction, CO 81506
(303) 879-6111
**PURGATORY SKI AREA**
P.O. Box 666; Durango, CO 81302 (303) 247-9000
**SILVER CREEK**
P.O. Box 4001; Silver Creek, CO 80446
(303) 887-3356; (1-800) 526-0590
**SKI COOPER**
P.O. Box 896; Leadville, CO 80461 (303) 486-3684
**SKI ESTES PARK**
P.O. Box 1379; Estes Park, CO 80517; (303) 586-4887
**SKI SUNLIGHT**
10901 County Rd. 117; Glenwood Springs, CO 81601
(303) 945-7491
**SNOWMASS RESORT ASSOCIATION**
P.O. Box 5566; Snowmass Village, CO 81615
(303) 923-2018; Toll free from Denver area: 892-7100
**SNOW MOUNTAIN RANCH / YMCA OF THE ROCKIES**
P.O. Box 169; Winter Park, CO 80482
(303) 887-2152; Toll free from Denver area: 443-4743
**STEAMBOAT SKI CORPORATION**
2305 Mt. Werner Circle; Steamboat
 Springs, CO 80487 (303) 879-6111
**TELLURIDE SKI RESORT, INC.**
P.O. Box 307; Telluride, CO 81435; (303) 728-3856
**UNITED STATES OLYMPIC COMMITTEE**
1750 E. Boulder St.; Colorado Springs, CO 80909
(303) 632-5551
**VAIL RESORT ASSOCIATION**
241 E. Meadow Dr.; Vail, CO 81657; Toll free from
Denver: 623-6624; (1-800) 525-3875; (303) 476-5677
**VISTA VERDE SKI RANCH**
P.O. Box 465; Steamboat Springs, CO 80477
(303) 879-3858
**WINTER PARK RESORT**
P.O. Box 36; Winter Park, CO 80482 (303) 726-5514
726-4101; Toll free from Denver area: 892-0961
**WOLF CREEK** (303) 264-2533
P.O.Box 1036; Pagosa Springs, CO 81147

United States Olympic Committee

# U.S. OLYMPIC COMMITTEE

The central coordinating body for Olympic-hopeful amateur athletes in the U.S. is headquartered in Colorado Springs. The U.S. Olympic Committee's purpose is to arrange funding, training and opportunities for athletes of all abilities, in preparation for possible Olympic participation. Through its governing bodies, USOC is responsible for selecting the teams which will represent the U.S. Ours is the only National Olympic Committee of the 160 in the world that does not receive financial support from the Federal Government, purposely to discourage government interference in the selection of athletes.

The main USOC training center is on 34 acres, where 12,000-15,000 athletes train each year. The committee provides living accommodations, and all the equipment necessary for training. Each summer in non-Olympic years, the U.S. Olympic Festival is held in various American cities. Nearly 3,000 athletes compete in 34 sports, with a special competition for disabled athletes. Since the first modern Olympic games in 1896, the U.S. has won more gold medals than any other country: 1,445. The winter Olympics, instituted in 1924, are held in the winter preceding the summer games.